The Glass Age

Also by Cole Swensen:

The Book of a Hundred Hands
Goest
Such Rich Hour
Oh
Try
Noon
Numen
Park
New Math
It's Alive She Says

Translations:
Ring Rang Wrong by Suzanne Doppelt
Physis by Nicolas Pesques
Colonel Zoo by Olivier Cadiot
Future Former Fugitive by Olivier Cadiot
Art Poetic' by Olivier Cadiot
OXO by Pierre Alferi
Natural Gaits by Pierre Alferi
Island of the Dead by Jean Fremon
Bayart by Pascalle Monnier

The Glass Age

Cole Swensen

Alice James Books

Farmington, Maine

10 9 8 7 6 5 4 3 2 1

Alice James Books are published by Alice James Poetry
Cooperative, Inc., an affiliate of the University of Maine
at Farmington.

Alice James Books
238 Main Street
Farmington, ME 04938

www.alicejamesbooks.org

Library of Congress Cataloging-in-Publication Data
Swensen, Cole
The glass age / Cole Swensen.
    p.   cm.
ISBN-13: 978-1-882295-60-9
ISBN-10: 1-882295-60-9
I. Title.
PS3569.W384G55 2007
811'.54—dc22   2006037929

Alice James Books gratefully acknowledges support
from the University of Maine at Farmington and the
National Endowment for the Arts. 🌱

Cover Art: Adrien Chancel, Detail from "Design for an
'Athenaeum for a Capital City'", 1877, courtesy École
nationale supérieure des beaux-arts

Acknowledgments

Grateful acknowledgment is made to the editors of the journals in which some of the following sections first appeared (sometimes in slightly different forms): *The American Poetry Review, Call, Canary, The Colorado Review, The New Review, 26d, No, Interim, 1913, Practice* and *42opus.*

To Bin Ramke and Jessica Munns
and all the Urquhart-Paps:
Jennifer, Robert, Marina, and Cat

Contents

The Open Window

◆

Pierre Bonnard, 1867–1947, painted next to a north-facing window. The battle over just what constitutes realism was at that moment particularly acute—an emotional thing, such as a cardinal out my window. Could streak away and shatter the composition of the world into a vivid wind in which the world goes astray.

Like most people, Bonnard painted

                           at that moment

               out my window

and across the street

                 most

          facing north, a cardinal first

is a color and might if

                 flight is

spliced into the eclipse outside my window, igniting patterns, parterres, some gardener
amiss.

or gardener of *is*

                    A window,
a necessary configuration of history and
I'm sorry, she said, turning
around so slowly
it turns out
                    (ash and sand)
and one too many
faces in the glass, they say

One if by glazed, etc. One if by
thy

ceilings are vaulted

and windows are painted into air

   which carries windows into your lungs, your blood, your brain.
He painted interiors. And then got to the ledge, the sill, the edge
on which sits a shell, and beyond, a dog out there in the yard,
and someone who turns away or toward

Sand and ash   (the ocean like glass
                    we say of a day when nothing moves)
further a natural feeling for light.

Bonnard's work implicitly asks what it is to see, and what it is to look through. We think of the arguments for the materiality of language that have played such an important role in philosophy and poetry since the beginning of the 20th century. Bonnard argued for a similar materiality of the window. There is nothing you can see through. You see

they say

    an entire world, they

    in a single grain

        and most of them,

        in retrospect, simply

They say to hold

Alfred Jarry

    in the street

        and turn him around

and say I will.

Glass is a neural construct that resembles a delta under glass.

Braided sand.

It was centuries before they got glass to let light in. Unlock it and reign. A slipper, a coffin, a difference in crystal.

In 1875 Caillebotte painted a man standing in a window, his back to us, looking down on a street in Paris. The image has become emblematic of enormous assumption—he who sees oversees, and yet is not seen in turn. Whereas Bonnard's windows have no one in them, unhindered ghost all over the crowded house.

Caillebotte anchored subjectivity in a single body, a faceless body, and no one we know. And so, he locks us out of the body, and the fragility that marks the 19th century wins.

Whereas a window with no one in it becomes a part of the body, with no seam between the continuous world that opens on touch. You hold it out at arm's length, and it hauls you onward, a mode of travel, distilling the senses in a glass vial, flying sleeves.

Sometimes Bonnard stood in the street and looked up at the lighted windows. In this way, he was never outside. He put real light in them and watched it dry. And though people walk back and forth behind these windows, we can't see them because they're indistinguishable from the windows themselves and from all that moves out from them on silent rails.

◆

A painting always has a model on its outside; it is always a window.
—Gilles Deleuze

When Leon Alberti published his *De Pictura* in 1435, he proposed the picture plane as an open window "through which I regard the scene . . ." through which the painting opens a world that was not there just seconds before.

And his carefully ruled and drafted *pavimenti,* in ways so like the paned window, now unattainable, to reach

is not necessarily to touch, and so on.

"The picture thus presented to a spectator in the Town Hall was curious and striking. It was an illuminated miniature, framed in by the dark margin of the window, the keen-edged shadiness of which emphasized by contrast the softness of the objects enclosed." Thomas Hardy, *Desperate Remedies,* 1871

describes the scene in which she watched her father fall to his death.

Leonardo da Vinci agreed completely: "Perspective is nothing other than seeing a place or objects behind a pane of glass," quite transparent, on the surface of which and into which objects sink,

                stain,

                        grave themselves in place

and shaped by distance— "therefore a painting

           will be the intersection

                  of a visual pyramid . . ."

Actual panes of glass were used for computing precise angles; hung before the artist's eyes, the world would strike a sudden proportion. Trace the line to the horizon with your finger across the clouded window. François I, watching his lover's carriage head off down the street, tracing her receding path on the pane with his diamond ring, and permanently engraved as if by accident, the glass remained obstinately flat, vertical, and reflected his own face back into a halved light, which happens, too, inside.

Landscape was also invented in 1435, when Robert Campin painted his home town and the fields beyond as seen through a window just behind the Madonna's right shoulder.

The space in paintings is not paint; it is space.

But unlike the *pavimenti*, the paned window cannot recede, and so
it ascends, tiled into sky

                        it climbs

                                   without diminution,

does not get smaller in the distance—
Rothkos, for instance.

◆

So many of Bonnard's paintings that seem to focus on windows are
actually more concerned with the frame. It stands in the way, not
framing the scene, but cutting it in two, thus framing not our view,
but our awareness of viewing,
our standing
                    in the middle and someone
who draws back a curtain,
                    who turns on a light,
who across the street
                    is more

given (with someone in them)

glancing out, you catch your neighbor's eye across the narrow

for an instant

            who turns on a light. To draw a thin line around. To say
outside is made of sun.

So often in Bonnard's work, the window is where we actually live, a vivid liminality poised on the sill, propped against the frame, he turns and speaks for the first time that day. The window, ajar, swings fully open in the breeze, and you watch his face glide away.

Such doors.

    The window falls
below the knee and rises higher than the raised hand.

Wittgenstein, determined to find
the window's perfect proportion, decided on ten to one,
height to width

but like a coastline,
a window is infinite, its perimeter
increasing forever without ever surpassing its frame

has everything to do with sight as exceeding. For centuries
they thought light

was something that flew out from the eye, the reaching child

                for centuries thought light

had everything to do
with a windowsill on which sits a shell.

Until Alhazen in the 10th century disproved it. Who also drew the first plan for a *camera obscura*, in which you use entire rooms to pull the entire world into you, my

Come to me in strands

"I am standing on a corner" (Bonnard to Charles Terrasse in a letter, 1927) "and objects close to me rise up toward my eyes."

who said Oh
how he loved yellow! could
make a man refract as if he too had passed

                                through matter cut
                            at just the right angle.

◆

Early photographs were taken with such long exposures that someone could walk through a room and become a vague streak of white against a window opening onto more light, and so on.

Photography replaced the river, which, due to unexpected comp-
lications, resulted in the Great Age of the Train. Bonnard started
photographing just as the snapshot became possible. Glass negatives
gave way to strips of film, and the river froze, intact. In shadow and
light, the Seine, said Marthe, standing in the garden, frame after
frame. We are multiplying the things we can and do see through.

We are walking across a room in front of a series of windows. The windows compose the entire wall, and the light floods in, separated only by the black borders of each frame.

Whoever crosses a lighted window makes it into a stage. Backlit, we're silhouettes, and thus take on the stilted gestures of characters projected by a magic lantern, where you make up the story yourself

as well as the people, one by one, because, unlike the picture plane—which is to say, the window looking out—the window looking in has only the foreground, and that, paper thin. The earliest movie was a window.

Bonnard was a great friend of the Lumière brothers, whose first film, *The Arrival of a Train in Ciotat Station,* showed in Paris in 1895. In it, you can see a woman in the last compartment with her face pressed to the window who makes no move as the train comes to a halt and all the passengers alight.

The earliest movie was a magic lantern; they'd slip panes of glass back and forth in front of the captive children on which were painted a woman, a wolf, a very, very small house inside your mind the walls go white. And when they once again coalesce, something lives in them.

There's something cinematic about Bonnard's compositions, each scene accentuating action, yet also decentralizing it, diffusing the focus into a plane that hums, a homogeneous intensity extending anarchically

which is echoed in its details—the pattern of the curtain coming in at the same scale as that of the variegated crops in the background and the tablecloth in the fore. It's an equivalent world, one in which each element serves as a clinamen to trip the homogeneity into precipitating specifics so numerous that they can construct a roiling chaos quite able to hurtle through darkness without a hitch.

Which can also be said of glass, with its random atomic arrangement, like that of a liquid, say, a river stopped mid-gesture, the blink that fixes the picture, suspending it on the surface, a permanent floating leaf.

Which became popularly known as *Ukioy-e,* the Floating World, our own daily one down here in all its drift—as opposed to the heavenly, locked in. Bonnard embraced the rage for this particular branch of Japanese aesthetics, which swept Europe during the late 19th century. But his interest went beyond stylistics; he was utterly devoted to the mundane. Those little objects that construct a table; the smaller ones that undo a window. The mail. It's the organizing principle of all his compositions, horizontal, looking neither up nor down, but out, and pushing the world continually outward, a floodplain on which skates, fleet apothecary, the glance.

◆

There's a person turning in the window—very small, very precise, invisible to the naked eye, turning and turning in the pane. In old glass, there is sometimes a tear in the window, sometimes a small bubble of air. Which itself has no frame. So where are you, the visitor, who came here to visit a painter?

H. H. Monroe, also known as Saki, in his story "The Open Window," has the hunters stride across the fields, hovering between worlds all headed toward a french door, and the visitor flees. Whatever enters through a window is a ghost; everything else is just visiting— transfixed witness to the instant of the threshold, the site of the slip, the shift; we look up.

So the ghost nips back, lands in the girl, though she doesn't know it yet; she thinks it's all a joke, and that everyone can see them striding across the lawn, and that the dog bounds along so high not because there's anything slightly too light about his form. She thinks the visitor is running from them, out there, who are running in, headlong, because even from across the field they can see that there's something terribly wrong with the girl. I must close the window, thought her aunt, entering from the salon. There's no point in leaving a window open in an empty room.

The Glass Act

♦

Vilhelm Hammershøi, 1864–1916, obsessively painted windows looking out on windows.

And painted through repeating glass doors that opened into rooms with nothing in them. Pale green on pale grey. The doors are often. They look into other rooms also open. He also painted women, often from the back, and often leaning over something in their laps, but he tended not to mix them with the windows.

"I see no difference," he said, "I have a nervous habit

of tracing a heart in his palm with his thumb.

Hammershøi made a room

a ship on its own
with panes overlapping all over the floor
the windows are drawn,

the windows come in   the windows come running

     and the open door is falling
               into room after room with the silence
of sun. He said open

and everything he painted then opened
a woman sewing
enters in infinite gradations, the white
that never gets there
remains
     who, alone in a house with light,
built his house entirely of doors.

◆

Bonnard painted a series from 1895 to '97 that also explores the potential of windows looking out on or into other windows.

When we see only the windows, there's something in them; when we also see the street, the windows are blank—something

has slipped, is now offset, and now the street and the windows comprise a single living thing, which makes it come out in color.

Bonnard: *Boulevard des Batignolles,* 1926. We are standing in a window looking out at windows. The windows on the other side are blind. They are on the other side. To look out is to see; to look in, to turn slowly white.

You have a choice: you can stand outside looking in, or inside looking out. It's one of those rare equivalences-in-difference. Bonnard stressed the difference, whereas Matisse was never convinced. "In my mind," said M. "they are one." Bonnard, *Dining Room*, 1944:

He is sitting in the garden at Le Bosquet. It's dark, and he's looking in on a yellow room, wondering how much of it is light, how much paint, and how does it thrive in the dark.

The next afternoon, Marthe is out in the yard and comes up to lean on the windowsill and calls to you

who are in a museum looking at the painting, and so turn to say

the face is a glass vase half a century away, empty and reflecting the empty garden of the world.

◆

Bonnard had a double fixation: saturated color and utter transparency. Not so much opposites as an immanent collision of the present until it's tangible. Cracked open to reveal at its center, a verb. A marrow of glass at the heart of every wall, early windows were sometimes made of bone, scraped. Shell. Alabaster skull.

By drenching glass in color, Bonnard split it lengthwise, prophetic, Gauguinic, flayed, and so ushered it into the 20th century, where the window finally came into its own—Wittgenstein's sister's house in Vienna, Duchamp's *Large Glass*, incandescent, a window is a magnet

for color, and as white is the presence of all colors, a window acts as an inverse prism, gathering the intense pigments of the fractured world back into an immanence of unrestricted light.

*I often see reflections cross
non-reflective surfaces*

They swept the light up from the floors and stored it in stone jars,
which by morning

                    What light has seen

the jars were empty

                     keeps no sketch

returned to quartz and so dispersed

                                   throughout the busy afternoon.

Bonnard saw in the window not a contradiction, but a solid object
that could lead you through itself in the dark.

In 1898, in the apartment of Claude Terrasse, Bonnard helped Alfred Jarry set up his Théâtre des Pantins and made him over three hundred marionettes for the revival of *Ubu Roi*. The Lumière brothers' early movies were still very much on his mind, in which the shadows on the walls, in which the gesture leaves a life. He worked a little more on the lights. He hand-carved their strings from ice. Jarry's 'Pataphysical masterpiece *The Exploits & Opinions of Dr. Faustroll* includes a chapter dedicated to Bonnard and titled "How One Obtained Canvas." In it, everything turns to gold including the eye and all seeing is seeing as

if there were enough light.

Glazier, Glazier

◆

The history of the window and the history of glass are not as hand-in-hand as one might think; in fact, the Middle English for window, "wind eyes," suggests that the former is named precisely for the lack of the latter. What child does not draw a house with windows on either side of a central front door and thereby discover the key to both repetitive dreams and the scaffold of her mind. There's a chimney to one side or the other. With that hand, she'll pick up the pencil. Another word for dream is "the walking rooms." We add extra windows. We look for a house with more windows. I ask the realtor, haven't you got something with a glassed-in porch.

And Bonnard, perhaps without intending it, returned to the
etymology, the percentage of "eye" that means "open in wind."
Devant la fenêtre au Grand-Lemps

                         (which does not mean

             great lamp) 1923,

                the open is the theme. We get used to it, this
young woman adjusting her hat

                    and beside her in the mirror, the gap
of the open window
where the eye of the painting must also be standing. Must, in fact,
be your face, and she's
looking right through it. Elsewhere

there's a similar gesture, so close
you'd find a photograph in a folded envelope years later there's
another child in the painting walking toward her, maybe pleading,
a profile in such anguish he may not have meant it, or did not, so
caught up
in painting, see

                walking
                from left to right across the proscenium
emptiness
of the openness, wringing his hands.

Glass is not a liquid, but a non-crystalline rigid, and the window made its first appearance in Rome around the year 100, when reviewers said, "of poor optical quality," yet those who wanted fissured sight were living twice and lifted. When I was a child, I had a glass kite. Said the child staring out the window of the speeding train.

Though the addition of manganese oxide made it clearer, window glass for centuries gave a distorted view of the world, and, as only kings and churches could afford it, grave social injustice was inevitable.

It seemed to waver; it seemed to turn
everything beyond it into grain.

It was precisely this infidelity that narrowed the distance between the window and art until the distortions themselves became worthy of framing.

Epitomized by the Claude glass—a darkened mirror carried by gentlepeople in the 18th century on their travels. Held up to a landscape, it would abstract and stylize the scene, turning it into a sepia sketch by Claude Lorrain. They were often framed in gold, and often used by artists themselves, who were thereby spared the world.

♦

And so began the Age of Glass, the first one named for a thing man-made, and the first one made to break. Anemic ghost that lives on salt, it was an accident of silicate that neatly held its own until it suddenly exploded around 1800.

For instance, the earliest arcades, the glass-ceilinged passages interlaced across Paris, were constructed from the beginning of the 19th century on

and on, all
gallery. Adapted from the grand houses of Italy and France, with their long halls in which their owners' treasures lay exposed under glass.

The great conservatories took off at about the same time—Chatsworth, Chiswick, and from there to the public garden. A palm house, an aviary, a passion for orchids swept the country.

While in France, they built whole mansions of glass;
called *orangeries* or *serres* or *vies*, a conservatory can be

made, paned, claimed

I grew a lemon from a forest of thieves. I grieve

still for the infinitesimal

difference between
what you can see and what you cannot see.

"I see no difference," he said, sifting from the right hand to the left.
I am deep in the house
where after all these clocks, there is only grass
and someone coming down the hall whistling a tune that sounds
like someone walking down a spiral stair.

The Crystal Palace was arguably the greatest glass house ever built; over a third of a mile long, covering 18 acres, and incorporating 900,000 square feet of glass, it was built for the Great Exhibition of 1851. And with it, an age. Moved to Sydenham in 1852, and enlarged. They used the words *nave* and *transept* to describe it, and *epoch* more than once. Brief, it burned first in 1866, though much of it survived for another 70 years, when it burned again, and lit up the countryside for miles around. Whole families gathered in armchairs, and read the evening papers with the lights off.

On the Crystal Palace, with elms in its midst: "You might think you were under the billows of some fabulous river"

in the words of an observer cited by A. Démy and repeated by W. Benjamin, who goes on to note: "An Englishman with a violent passion for flowers insisted on seeing the whole place become a garden."

The great exposition ended. We remember the Thames, but not as a sequence

and then the Seine.

A ceiling paved in aquatic light—the arcades made it seem to come from somewhere else, its source lost and its substance filtered, falling in stains like leaves and clearing, and in the clearing, someone rests,

the extension of space by means of glass,

in the Crystal Palace, they left the trees .

The extension of glass by other means.

The origin of all architecture is the greenhouse (we begin

in shelter). For everything that can be counted,
there is a mean, and we end in balance, looking over the edge
to the opening half. And even then
the roof is made of glass.

And in inverted sympathy, Hullam Jones invented the glass-bottom boat in 1878 to bring the sky around, to fill a lightbulb with a sea, my glass ceiling besieged. It's rare but there's a species of gingko whose leaves are shaped as sails. That yet can levitate to any harbor, and from any harbor, find any other.

◆

Glass to glass. It makes of the fragile
an eyebone
              and why not entire
who could have won wars
                   could have

stopped on the surface, a series
of mirrors of Marthe sliding into a bath.

Which anchors, colors
waver
A woman bends down to pick up something we can't see. *Nude in an Interior*, c. 1935, washed with the light and air of an exterior world. She is bending down to touch something; and then she'll straighten up to look outside, and the hand will slip out of the hand as if someone forgot and let go of the body.

A window is always relative to a body, and the body is never repeated. Thus proliferates. Because every body involves a window or windows, looking out on the world "at large," as they say, the body is not single. And though painting was invented to correct this, it has ended up accomplishing the opposite, making the eye an errant thing, like that mode of traveling based on forgetting, which we also call "the body," so that these windows bring us back, but not to us.

◆

For a few years in the 1890s, Bonnard shared a studio with Vuillard, who also loved windows. Who wrote later from Passy, 1904, "windows I couldn't have hoped for," and painted *Florist's Garden* or *Par la fenêtre*, looking down onto and into greenhouses, which recalled Bonnard's *Some Aspects the City of Paris* until 1908, when he moved back to Clichy, and from his new window in the Place Vintimille, with its park, and Vuillard watches, carefully, tree by tree. A park is a distillation, every vagrant errant made topiary, entire migrations compressed in a sole parterre.

Vuillard sees it from above because he's living on the fourth floor, and every day the same women come with their children who have changed.

◆

Bonnard's antecedents included Mallarmé's "Les Fenêtres," with its *galleys of gold, beautiful as swans*

                in which the arc

                        into which

we walk. Geometry with imprecision at its heart
as the circle always veers in its infinity. Necessity. A man stands in his room and looks straight through. Who'd gotten old as he turned to see and saw the sun hitting stone, and heard a man calling "*Glaaazier Glaaazier*" down in the street below.

Baudelaire also wrote a poem titled "Les Fenêtres," in which
derrière une vitre
vit la vie
in which another's life takes over, and light must pass through it as
though expected.

          A window always marks the meeting of edges.
You might stumble.

For Mallarmé, a window looked outward; whereas Baudelaire's
looked back, somehow a part of the glance, they mean.

Whereas Bonnard managed, through adamant insistence, through
window after window, through sheer repetition, to keep them from
doing any such thing.

A life-sized window is the size of a life.

There is nothing more said Baudelaire, and here
inserted
numerous
adjectives
than a window lighted by a single candle. The flame at that distance resembles a face, which glances out, then turns away. The profile cuts the light in half. As the face, now only half in this world, builds a half-world on the other side, claimed Bonnard, any face is half a world away. And waits.

mysterious
prolific
shadowy
dazzling—by a single candle. *In that black or luminous square,*
Baudelaire crossed the room and closed the window. There is
sand on fire, and we stray.

Early windows had no glass. They were gaps until shuttered, at
which point they went back to being walls. They'd paint faces
on the shutters and open them by calling out their names. This

changed the human body, changed it to a gate, which is a
breach. Jan Dibbets recorded the sunlight coming in through the
windows of a gallery for an entire day, how it crossed the floor

in a broad, slow sweep, one frame an hour, a carnival of poise.
What one can see out there in the daylight is always less.

Apollinaire, writing much later, saw a train in snow and flashing
   The window opens like an orange
   The lovely fruit of light
                              saw the yellow die
in perfect squares, and still the thriving snow, one eye closed
as if lining up
an object nearby
with one in the distance, and the other eye closed as if
momentarily suspended from a great height.

Apollinaire's poem "Les Fenêtres" was published in the catalogue
for the 1913 Berlin exhibition of Robert Delaunay's window
paintings—*Windows on the City, Simultaneous Windows, Windows
Opened Simultaneously*

              whose studies in color suggested the splinter

            whose affection for Bergson, who said the succession
of our states of consciousness
when the "I" lets live

           in through the skin
gently, Delaunay believed
that the eye alone, half planet, half brain, could face the world
entire, simultaneous,

          we the unperished,
we shatter
into patterns

        counting threads. .

◆

Every window implies a blind spot—it's the air, the percentage of air in every scene; the portion that can't be seen lying over everything. The unveiled veil.

Alberti also created a veil, one of threads to aid the student in establishing correct perspective, but explicitly stated that this was really a sort of window without glass.

One of Bonnard's last paintings is titled *The Small Window* and shows, through an open window that frames three sides of the painting, another window, red, and at a distance, a suggestion of a building or maybe by now a window alone, a thriving shore.

"The most beautiful things in museums are the windows," he said, looking out at the Seine from the Louvre, June, 1946.

Notes

The quotations on page 56 are from *The Arcades Project* by Walter Benjamin. The italicized second line on page 64 is from Mallarmé's poem "Les Fenêtres." The italicized passages on pages 65–67 are from Baudelaire's poem "Les Fenêtres." The italicized passage on page 68 is from Apollinaire's poem "Les Fenêtres."

Recent Titles from **Alice James Books**

The Case Against Happiness, Jean-Paul Pecqueur
Ruin, Cynthia Cruz
Forth A Raven, Christina Davis
The Pitch, Tom Thompson
Landscapes I & II, Lesle Lewis
Here, Bullet, Brian Turner
The Far Mosque, Kazim Ali
Gloryland, Anne Marie Macari
Polar, Dobby Gibson
Pennyweight Windows: New & Selected Poems, Donald Revell
Matadora, Sarah Gambito
In the Ghost-House Acquainted, Kevin Goodan
The Devotion Field, Claudia Keelan
Into Perfect Spheres Such Holes Are Pierced, Catherine Barnett
Goest, Cole Swensen
Night of a Thousand Blossoms, Frank X. Gaspar
Mister Goodbye Easter Island, Jon Woodward
The Devil's Garden, Adrian Matejka
The Wind, Master Cherry, the Wind, Larissa Szporluk
North True South Bright, Dan Beachy-Quick
My Mojave, Donald Revell
Granted, Mary Szybist
Sails the Wind Left Behind, Alessandra Lynch
Sea Gate, Jocelyn Emerson
An Ordinary Day, Xue Di
The Captain Lands in Paradise, Sarah Manguso
Ladder Music, Ellen Doré Watson
Self and Simulacra, Liz Waldner
Live Feed, Tom Thompson
The Chime, Cort Day
Pity the Bathtub Its Forced Embrace of the Human Form, Matthea Harvey
The Arrival of the Future, B.H. Fairchild
The Art of the Lathe, B.H. Fairchild

Alice James Books has been publishing exclusively poetry since 1973. One of the few presses in the country that is run collectively, the cooperative selects manuscripts for publication through both regional and national annual competitions. New regional authors become active members of the cooperative, participating in the editorial decisions of the press. The press, which historically has placed an emphasis on publishing women poets, was named for Alice James, sister of William and Henry, whose fine journal and gift for writing went unrecognized within her lifetime.

Typeset and Designed by Mike Burton

Printed by Thomson-Shore
on 50% postconsumer recycled paper
processed chlorine-free